# ARE CIVIL RIGHTS

## ON LIFE SUPPORT?

Are Civil Rights on Life Support? © 2011 by Sam Maze

ISBN 13: 978-1-934556-38-2
Library of Congress Control Number: 2011935391

Published by:
**ZLPI**
Zoe Life Publications, Inc. ~ www.zlpi.us

Post Office Box 310096
Fontana, CA 92331
1~888~ZOE~ZLPI

Editor: Nancy Deyo
Cover Design: TABIA Graphics

Printed in the United States of America

# ARE CIVIL RIGHTS

## ON LIFE SUPPORT?

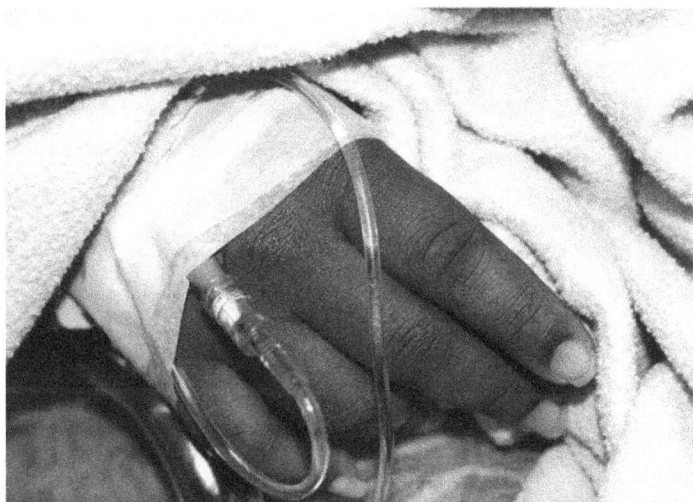

# SAM MAZE

ZOE LIFE PUBLICATIONS, INC.

CALIFORNIA

# TABLE OF CONTENTS

## ACKNOWLEDGEMENTS

I would like to take this opportunity to thank those who were instrumental in fulfilling my desire to write a book that will hopefully someday raise the eyebrows and thoughts of people everywhere to effect positive change for each and every individual. I am particularly thankful for my publisher, Mrs. Starla Porter, who gave me the support needed to move forward. I dedicate this book to one of my early Mentors, the late Dennis Callahan, EEO Manager, who taught me the understanding of Equal Employment Opportunity; Mr. Norm Hensley, one of the few Black Directors that worked for the Department of Veterans Affairs; Mr. Gerald Hinch, a prior National Washington DC EEO Officer for Federal Agencies; my loving wife, Samira Maze, who supported me and encouraged me in times of challenge; and most of all, my loving and dear children (Tammy, LaShanda, Jennell, Terrell and Jovan) who inspired me to write for a better world and future; and without question, my God and Savior from Whom all my blessings flow.

The Author of this book and/or any individual identified with remarks, comments, opinions or other statements, are not responsible for the misinterpretation or misuse of the information. This information is based on actual experiences, awareness and involvement of the subject matter. We disclaim any responsibility or liability related to this book.

The information provided in this book is not a substitute for the advice of your attorney or other qualified legal professional. Always seek the advice of your attorney or other qualified legal professional with any questions you may have regarding civil rights or equal employment opportunity. Never disregard professional legal advice or delay in seeking it because of something you have read in this book.

# INTRODUCTION

When we are faced with what appears to be an insurmountable situation, we can choose to adapt, accept or suffer. The success of the Civil Rights movement was one of the most challenging achievements for anyone in the history of mankind. Through the voices of those who, despite the risk involved, had the courage to speak up and speak out, we were able to overcome the fangs of oppression and unfairness to some degree in the work world. Civil Rights laws gave hope and a sense of self-worth and fairness that should have already existed in the workplace, an accomplishment that was amazing in itself. The Civil Rights Act of 1964, the Equal Pay Act, the Age Discrimination Employment Act, the EEO Reform Act, Rehabilitation Act of 1973, Americans with Disabilities Act and Executive Orders were laws that we well know originated from the bold and brave leaders like Dr. Martin Luther King, Jr., the group marches of people from all backgrounds, and many others who opposed illegal discrimination. Several events and court cases set precedents for fair and equitable treatment in the work world. Having the right to work in a job for which you are the best qualified was quite an achievement during that needed change. I am honored to continue documenting this book during this 25th Annual Holiday of Dr. Martin Luther King, Jr., Monday, January 17, 2011.

As we discuss this significant topic, let us think about what people are experiencing today: Ruling by Fear and Sell- Outs; the Courage to Effect Change; Utilizing Resources and Working Together; Enhancing Accountability; and How to Proceed in the New Decade. Have you noticed what is going on today in the work world as it relates to fairness, the right to achieve and the fear of retaliation? More importantly, have you observed the lack of understanding or the need to support Leadership that would make a positive difference to create a more productive and comfortable work environment? There are many things happening in the workplace today. Civil Rights are experiencing a shortness of breath; trembling and nausea are setting in; its heart is murmuring and its eyes are dilated. Is this the end? The sirens are loud and the lights are flashing. It reaches the point when help is essential. Are Civil Rights on life support? The question is, what have you seen over the years? Where are we now? Have you really noticed what is going on?

## HAVE YOU NOTICED WHAT IS GOING ON?

As we ponder the things that are happening today, we must reflect on what we have been through, where and why has it changed from fairness and equity to power and fear. The need of some for power has always existed, but one would think that true power is having the ability to be followed and respected by others, willingly and without force. In the current economy, it is great to have a job but it is truly amazing how organizations have mastered (or think they have mastered) the art of discriminating legally and ignoring the basic civil rights of individuals. People are expected to come to work, keep their mouths shut and their noses to the grindstone, if you will. It has travelled full circle to become a performance like the three monkeys' "see no evil," "hear no evil," and "speak no evil." Not only people are being treated without respect, but coworkers are afraid to speak up and witness for them because they do not want to lose their jobs. Some of this is based on the paradigm that exists in the workplace, just as Stephen Covey indicated in his book, "Seven Habits of Highly Effective People" about the paradigms of thinking.

People think win-lose, lose-win, lose-lose, win-win or no deal. As a Covey Facilitator for my employer, I learned that Covey talked about how people in society learn to be competitive as they grow into adults. Most of everything we do involves some kind of competition, getting the highest grades, being the best on the sports teams, having the most beautiful boy or girlfriend or the best looking car. This is not specifically what Covey stated but it is the gist of my understanding of his reference. Therefore, most people are conditioned to think win-lose, meaning that I win and you lose. That mentality is what I have noticed in the workplace

11

today. Instead of putting forth stronger efforts into learning why people believe they are mistreated or discriminated against, organizations take the position that they must win every case or every complaint. They will do anything to achieve that goal, even if that means misrepresenting the truth or fabricating evidence. The same can be said for complainants or frivolous filers, focusing on beating the organization even though they know they are wrong. I recall a case in which a manager had strong evidence of discriminatory behavior and filed a complaint. He had emails, documents, witnesses and past practices of the responsible official. The Personnel Representative assigned to the case was a known alcoholic with a reputation of being win-lose without exception. The organization head had an opportunity to deal with the situation early on but maintained this win-lose mentality, waiting until the case was ready to go before the judge before offering a settlement of hundreds of thousands of dollars. It helped me understand the logic in how workplace management currently demonstrates that they are the rulers, have the power and do not have to respect individual civil rights.

It is breathtaking to realize that we can be in one place in the world, yet we can talk to and interact with another nation miles away. Our technology has taken us to areas far beyond our greatest expectations with more still to come. We can be at a business meeting in London and start our cars in San Francisco. We can stretch our imaginations way beyond ourselves to a zone that gives us peace or tranquility, even as our immediate challenges rage in turmoil. We can make a deposit into our children's account without even being near them. But for some strange reason, we cannot make a simple deposit into the hearts and emotions of everyone who is different from us. Why is it that our first thoughts are selfish? Of course, this does not apply to all, but one individual is enough to create a break in the thread of humanity that says "no matter what, we are all in this thing together." Why is it that we can do so many things but when it comes to basic fairness, service to others and compassion for those who are less fortunate, we seem to grab hold of greed, selfishness and power? Have you noticed that some will do anything to feel in charge when the greatest of us throughout history have served their fellow men and women to build a better world?

In the workplace, it is so evident that people that have authority and even some who do not seem to abuse that authority. What a great working world we would have, if we could take the same effort we direct toward enhancing technology and put it toward human care and basic equality. The lowliest position in the organization should be treated with the most respect because that is where it all starts. It is not all management's fault, but leadership plays a tremendous role in the dynamics and culture of an organization. What can be done?

# MANAGEMENT'S ROLE IN PREVENTING DISCRIMINATION

What can management do to help prevent discrimination and the perception of discrimination? There are several ways to address this issue. Many times, the culture of an organization starts with the leadership paradigm. How does management create a trustworthy workplace that is equal to all if the practices and expectations are not conducive to an environment of fairness? In an organization, the leadership must promote fairness and equity in all of their actions. There must be an expectation that all will be treated with respect. Although it's a simple word, it has a monumental meaning, both in the workplace or in life in general. Having respect for those for whom you work and those who work for you is one of the most effective ways to prevent perceptions of discrimination. People vary and respect may mean something different in different ways to each individual. Having open communication whereby people are not afraid to express themselves in the appropriate manner contributes to an environment of awareness and trust.

Management has the authority and responsibility to demonstrate practices of fairness. How can leadership be fair if they do not know what subordinates are thinking or experiencing? Creating and maintaining an open door policy is more than just a phrase; leaders must leave no doubt that they are approachable and they are to both listen and understand. All too often, the expectation is that you will do your job and then go home without causing any problems. That may work in a perfect world, but people have many things going on in their lives that affect their daily interactions at work. Having a manager that every employee can talk to and who is willing to listen is one of the basic trust factors that underlie perceptions of care and fairness. Now, it is a terrible thing when an individual shares information and, by the time they get to the cafeteria, their business is divulged throughout the organization. That will definitely create distrust and a perception of differential treatment during critical times. Of course, it may not be possible to have everyone willingly sit down and communicate, but it is possible to display a listening ear and concerned spirit. The basic job of some managers may be to direct and guide, but some actually get down into the trenches with their employees to demonstrate that they will not ask for something to be done that they are not willing to do themselves. That can inspire great respect in times of deadlines and crises. To know that I have a manager who will work side by side with me means the entire world. I may not be so quick to perceive treatment as discriminatory when leadership has demonstrated a mentality of teamwork, regardless of their position title.

In this current work world, time is money and we have gotten so caught up in on-line training. If you think about it, time spent on detailed, effective training will no doubt save the organization money and time. Management has requirements and develops a computer program to address those requirements. Leaders whiz through the material, probably only remembering the few points that caught their interest. We need to get back to the Nitty-Gritty of one-on-one, hands-on training where leaders can learn about things that cause complaints and ways to prevent them, not to mention vital areas like effective communication, diversity awareness and good sound management practices. All it takes to paralyze an organization's ability to function is one misunderstanding that develops into a major complaint.

Some things are based on our own biases and beliefs. For example, in one case, the leader (Director) was presented with allegations which were basically substantiated with evidence. However, the Director was so accustomed to thinking win-lose that he ignored the writing on the wall. His perception was to win every case at any cost, not realizing that sometimes winning no matter the cost is actually losing. Management will get more out of employees when they believe that they are cared about and have value, and are treated the same or at least equal to others. In another situation, a position became open which offered an opportunity for advancement. A few employees were in place that could fill the position temporarily until it was announced and a selection was made. The manager assigned one of her employees to temporarily fill the position, not only because this individual had the knowledge, skills and abilities to do the job, but also because this individual was always catering to the manager and gave no back talk or challenge when it came to being assigned duties. However, the other employees did not have a chance to rotate into the vacant position, putting them at a disadvantage when the application and interviewing process took place. I need not say that the circumstances inspired at least three complaints of discrimination. Although the manager was comfortable with the chosen employee, there was a responsibility to give all an opportunity to rotate through the position, putting them on an equal footing when they submitted their applications.

Many times in reasonable accommodation cases, management attempts to make decisions in a vacuum without expertise input. One of the most common reasons for an accusation of discrimination based on a disability is the failure of management to communicate and interact with an employee to obtain a better understanding of their needs. Establishing a committee is a very helpful tool with which companies can address disability concerns, but a committee is not the total answer. The committee must be timely and effective. If a Human Resources Labor Management individual is chairing that committee, it could have the appearance of unfairness because the role of that chair is to protect management. The organization's chairperson should be someone chairing that is neither pro management nor pro employee and he or she must be trained thoroughly to lead such a committee.

So what can management do to help prevent discrimination? It starts with respecting their staff and themselves. Understanding their biases, weaknesses and strengths will have an effect on the way in which they lead. Management must think critically about their approach to situations and how that approach might be perceived. Training opportunities that are not "one size fits all", but instead provide extensive one-on-one or hands-on training will provide them with the long lasting tools to perform their duties. Difficult employees must be dealt with. You cannot allow one employee to continuously come in late and reprimand another because they do not say how high when you say jump. Most importantly, good sound leadership fairness and concern about the people who support your right to be a leader and manager should be practiced. It starts with leadership.

Nobody in their right state of mind thinks that leadership, supervising or managing is easy. During his time, the great Dr. Martin Luther King, Jr. indicated that leadership is serving. The best leaders serve their staff and to say the least, serving or leading is sometimes difficult. For example, you may not want to counsel that employee with a problem because you do not want to confront the issue. Everything seems fine, so why rock the boat? Or you know an individual or group is out of line and, instead of documenting the incidents, you just let it go because you have a good heart. Actually, you are doing a disservice to both those employees and the other workers when you do not deal with the matter up front. Supervisors must document, document and document. I have seen some cases of the supervisor saying, "Enough is enough," and they were right. However, they had no documentation to support them when they addressed their concerns and did not give the staff member an opportunity to change. He or she says, "I did not know it was a problem until today," and a third party asks the question, "When did you write all of this up?" If the answer is just a couple of days ago, you have just set the employee up all in one step. Where was the progressive discipline, guidance and leadership? The key is to do the same for one individual as you would do for another in similar circumstances. If it is not in writing, it more than likely did not happen. That does not mean go for the jugular vein at the first opportunity. If the situation is appropriate, you can change behavior with a verbal counseling, while more critical situations may require more serious actions.

Always seek advice from your human resources contacts. Most organizations have labor contacts, either in human resources or named in the union-negotiated contract. It is appropriate to meet with the union before you make a decision that may violate the contract. Up front communication is much better than an explanation on the back end that may not be substantiated or could be incorrect. Be diligent, fair and talk with those who have travelled the road, not those who have a bone to pick. Just because another leader had a challenge with an employee does not mean that you will. However, past behavior is a good indicator of the type of employee you have. Know your staff. You can do a great deal to prevent perceptions of discrimination or unfair treatment.

One major area of concern is sexual harassment; management must have a zero-tolerance policy on this type of behavior. One bad decision or one case of sexual harassment can ruin the reputation of an organization. Who would want to be a customer or even work at an organization who would tolerate this type of behavior? The EEOC which, as you should know by now, is the Equal Employment Opportunity Commission that enforces civil rights laws. Let's look at some situations I created for you.

## MANAGEMENT SITUATIONS:

1. You are the Manager in a Supply Section with approximately five employees; they all differ in terms of race, sex, national origin and age. A couple of them work very hard but like to joke while they work. One of them is your best employee who does anything you ask and watches your back when you are away. Another one is frequently late and is a little sarcastic towards you. The one that watches your back is also late more often than they should be. When the sarcastic, continually tardy employee has basically gotten on your last nerve, if you will, you decide you are going to deal with him. To establish that you have no tolerance for his attitude and lateness so you decide to discipline him. He files a discrimination complaint because he feels that he is treated differently from your office pet, who is of a different race and sex. What should you do?

A. Withdraw the disciplinary action and give a warning.

B. Document all of the problems you have had with him and give the information to Human Resources.

C. Tell him that the office pet also received a disciplinary action for being late.

D. Contact Equal Employment Opportunity and Human Resources for advice, and establish a policy of expecting all employees to adhere to the attendance rules; deal with the sarcastic attitude as a separate issue.

2. You are the immediate supervisor of a staff of 10, all of whom are good employees. One employee has a disability and needs a little assistance from time to time. You noticed her struggling to complete the essential functions of her job. An inspection is coming up and your boss tells you that he does not want her in the area when the inspectors arrive. Your boss displays his insensitivity to people with disabilities, saying he doesn't care what you do but to get her out of there. You tell your boss that it is both unfair and illegal to deal with the situation in that manner. Your boss tells you to find a way or else. What should you do?

A. Tell your boss, "Hell no; go shove it."

B. Ask the disabled employee to take off a couple of days until the inspection is over.

C. Be proactive and ask the disabled employee, if there is an accommodation that would help her complete the essential functions of her job.

D. Let your boss know that you are uncomfortable with the request and that you will talk with his boss as well as Human Resources about what to do.

E. Stand up for what you believe is right and deal with your boss through the proper channels.

3. You are the top leader at an organization. Your headquarters has publicly announced a million dollar award for all subordinate organizations that develop operational support demonstrating effective diversity enhancement programs; fairness and equity to all employees, supervisors and managers' and a promotion program that reaches those of all backgrounds. You must validate this through an effective report submitted for review. What should you do?

A. Have a discussion about preparing a report that would win the reward with Human Resources and Equal Employment Opportunity Commission representative.

B. Because your organization needs the funds to increase your operational capabilities, ask the appropriate staff to put together programs that appear to have been already in place and that will continue to operate.

C. Follow up with the officials you have already charged with implementing and maintaining programs of this nature to capture what they have already done and what they plan to do in the future. Put together the supportive statistical data to demonstrate your efforts. Emphasize the low complaint numbers and the diverse promotions that have taken place.

## Sexual Harassment

It is unlawful to harass a person (an applicant or employee) because of that person's sex. Harassment can include "sexual harassment" or unwelcome sexual advances, requests for sexual favors, and other verbal or physical harassment of a sexual nature.

Harassment does not have to be of a sexual nature; however, it can include offensive remarks about a person's sex. For example, it is illegal to harass a woman by making offensive comments about women in general.

Both victim and the harasser can be either a woman or a man, and the victim and harasser can be the same sex.

Although the law doesn't prohibit simple teasing, offhand comments, or isolated incidents that are not very serious, harassment is illegal when it is so frequent or severe that it creates a hostile or offensive work environment or when it results in an adverse employment decision (such as the victim being fired or demoted).

The harasser can be the victim's supervisor, a supervisor in another area, a co-worker, or someone who is not an employee of the employer, such as a client or customer.

Another area management and employees of which should be aware is religious discrimination. Let's take a look at what EEOC has to say about that. *"The EEOC provides the following information through their website www.EEOC.us and deserves the credit for this technical information about discrimination."*

## Religious Discrimination

Religion discrimination involves treating a person (an applicant or employee) unfavorably because of his or her religious beliefs. The law protects not only people who belong to traditional, organized religions, such as Buddhism, Christianity, Hinduism, Islam, and Judaism, but also others who have sincerely held religious, ethical or moral beliefs.

Religious discrimination can also involve treating someone differently because that person is married to (or associated with) an individual of a particular religion or because of his or her connection with a religious organization or group.

## Religious Discrimination & Work Situations

The law forbids discrimination when it comes to any aspect of employment, including hiring, firing, pay, job assignments, promotions, layoff, training, fringe benefits, and any other term or condition of employment.

## Religious Discrimination & Harassment

It is illegal to harass a person because of his or her religion. Harassment can include, for example, offensive remarks about a person's religious beliefs or practices. Although the law doesn't prohibit simple teasing, offhand comments, or isolated incidents that aren't very serious, harassment is illegal when it is so frequent or severe that it creates a hostile or offensive work environment or when it results in an adverse employment decision (such as the victim being fired or demoted). The harasser can be the victim's supervisor, a supervisor in another area, a co-worker, or someone who is not an employee of the employer, such as a client or customer.

## Religious Discrimination & Reasonable Accommodation

The law requires an <u>employer or other covered entity</u> to reasonably accommodate an employee's religious beliefs or practices, unless doing so would cause more than a minimal burden on the operations of the employer's business. This means an employer may be required to make reasonable adjustments to the work environment that will allow an employee to practice his or her religion.

Examples of some common religious accommodations include flexible scheduling, voluntary shift substitutions or swaps, job reassignments, and modifications to workplace policies or practices.

## Religious Accommodation/Dress & Grooming Policies

Unless it would be an undue hardship on the employer's operation of its business, an employer must reasonably accommodate an employee's religious beliefs or practices. This applies not only to schedule changes or leave for religious observances, but also to such things as dress or grooming practices that an employee has for religious reasons. These might include, for example, wearing particular head coverings or other religious dress (such as a Jewish yarmulke or a Muslim headscarf), or wearing certain hairstyles or facial hair (such as Rastafarian dreadlocks or Sikh uncut hair and beard). It also includes an employee's observance of a religious prohibition against wearing certain garments (such as pants or miniskirts).

When an employee or applicant needs a dress or grooming accommodation for religious reasons, he should notify the employer that he needs such an accommodation for religious reasons. If the employer reasonably needs more information, the employer and the employee should engage in an interactive process to discuss the request. If it would not pose an undue hardship, the employer must grant the accommodation.

## Religious Discrimination & Reasonable Accommodation & Undue Hardship

An employer does not have to accommodate an employee's religious beliefs or practices if doing so would cause undue hardship to the employer. An accommodation may cause undue hardship if it is costly, compromises workplace safety, decreases workplace efficiency, infringes on the rights of other employees, or requires other employees to do more than their share of potentially hazardous or burdensome work.

## Religious Discrimination and Employment Policies/Practices

An employee cannot be forced to participate (or not participate) in a religious activity as a condition of employment.

# RULING BY FEAR

As an Equal Employment Opportunity Complaint Investigator and EEO Program Manager, I recollect several situations involving perspective witnesses who had knowledge of incidents substantiating illegal discriminatory behavior, but who were afraid to testify because they believed they would be targeted for retaliation or reprisal. This has become very common in the workplace, and this trend has clearly become a matter of fear. Now, all managers and supervisors or leaders are not, if you will, control freaks, but there are a few. One insensitive, biased leader could be all that is necessary to create an environment of fear and distrust. At this time, people come to work with a mentality of minding their own business, even as they see mistreatment and the violation of individual civil rights happen before their eyes. There are some organizations that practice the harassment and non-promotion of individuals who file complaints, serve as witnesses for others who file complaints, or who voice their issues with discriminatory treatment.

In one case, an EEO Manager whose role was to remain neutral and provide information and advice to concerned individuals was escorted off station, sending a chill throughout the company; the intent was to communicate to other employees, "Look at what we can do if you support civil rights." Imagine the fear that this could create in the other employees. Ruling by Fear sends a subliminal message that affects the minds and courage of people who would otherwise stand up against this type of organizational climate. It is amazing how a small number of people have such courage while others choose to not get involved, even though the very same thing could happen to them. In another situation, several supervisors wanted to file a class complaint because, although their duties had increased, they had received no compensation such as promotions for their additional work. They were advised to attempt resolution because there were not enough numbers involved for a class. One of the supervisors was told privately that if they filed an EEO complaint, they would be in trouble and get nothing.

Although there are quite a few good organizations with good leaders, the fear factor still plays a significant role in the comfort and well-being of employees, including managers and supervisors. Some managers and supervisors are afraid to be fair to their staff because of the expectations of their leadership. Why are some leaders afraid to just be fair and appropriate? Well, as you know, some of our built-in perceptions of being "better than," our biases of different are superior; and our need for power cause that competitive mentality that has the effect of holding others down. Filling the atmosphere with fear is a way for some to feel more comfortable while it actually exhibits the coward within them which is rooted in insecurity. So it may not be that the immediate supervisor is the problem but rather that the top management personnel wants to keep everyone in line through fear tactics. We must make the decision to be unafraid to stand up for our rights and the rights of others. One noteworthy experience I had as an EEO Specialist occurred when a Service Manager had several EEO complaints filed against him. He was known as a hard-nosed, insensitive, inflexible leader so people were forced to file in EEO as a reaction to his style and treatment. Low and behold, one day he stopped by my office. He sat down and said he wanted to file an EEO complaint because his manager was trying to fire him and was treating him terribly. I had to regard him in the same way as all of the employees that had complained about him. That was something I could never forget.

One of the important points is that ruling by fear is only effective if individuals or groups allow it to happen. It starts with you; if you give the impression that you can be bullied, hoodwinked and bamboozled, you promote ruling by fear behavior. Is your grass green enough to say that "there is no grounds to come after me so I have every right to challenge, complain or dispute how I am being mistreated and my civil rights are being violated"? For example, you cannot be late for work four days out of the week, be off every other Friday and Monday during the year, and then file a discrimination complaint because of your race. Correction, you can file but you will not prevail because of your behavior, which management has every right to address.

Let's also be fair. All managers, supervisors or leaders are not supporters of this tactic nor do they, as individuals, want to instill fear in their employees. Some may be following command directives and some have the courage to serve those who work for them. During my career, I've met a few that demonstrated a clear and convincing concern about their subordinate's welfare. When I was in the military, I had a Commander who was a great role model for me. He was a white male and showed no indication of being a racist or unfair. I learned a great deal just by watching him and following his leadership practices. I recall a time when the military was emphasizing the fitness and best qualified expectations of all and I had to complete my 2 mile run within the allocated time frame. I hated long distance running and was pretty discouraged. I was far overseas and felt alone, but I had to complete this task or face being sent home. My commander looked me in the eye and said, you can do it; I know you can. Get out there and get it done. He was easy to talk to and I trusted him. Needless to say, with that additional encouragement, I got it done with flying colors. Managers or leaders that support their staffs can get them to do anything for them without hesitation, just as I was ready to go to war for that commander. When you have a leadership responsibility, your treatment of subordinates can go a long way. Perceptions of unfair treatment and discrimination usually stem from distrust and inconsistent or questionable behavior. So ruling by fear should not be an automatic response, even if you have experienced that from some other supervisors.

This would be a good point to take a look at statistics. There are numbers found on the EEOC website that can give you an idea of trends and practices. Let's see what we found. What do the numbers demonstrate in your opinion? Have we gotten better? Can ruling by fear or control play a part in the statistics presented? One thing is certain; if the numbers are correct (and I have no reason to believe they are not), they paint a picture of what we have experienced over the years.

In my review of the statistics presented by EEOC (the Equal Employment Opportunity Commission) at this website http://www.eeoc.gov/eeoc/statistics/nofear/nofear.cfm under the title "Equal Employment Opportunity Data Posted Pursuant to the No Fear Act," I found these statistics to share with you.

Equal Employment Opportunity Data Posted Pursuant to Title III of the Notification and Federal Employee Antidiscrimination and Retaliation Act of 2002 (No FEAR Act), Pub. L. 107-174

## Number of Complaints Filed:

Equal Employment Opportunity Data Posted Pursuant to Title III of the Notification and Federal Employee Antidiscrimination and Retaliation Act of 2002 (No FEAR Act), Pub. L. 107-174

| Complaint Activity Sec. 1614.704 (a), (b), and (c) | Comparative Data (Sec. 1614.705) | | | | | | | | | 2011 thru 06/30/11 |
|---|---|---|---|---|---|---|---|---|---|---|
| | Previous Fiscal Year Data | | | | | | | | | |
| | '02 | '03 | '04 | '05 | '06 | '07 | '08 | '09 | '10 | |
| Number of Complaints Filed | 46 | 39 | 33 | 26 | 21 | 28 | 37 | 30 | 33 | 13 |

This depicts complaints filed at EEOC that began in 2002 at 48 and decreased to 21 complaints by year 2006. They started increasing more to 37 complaints in 2008. They settled down to 33 in 2010 and as of this review in July of 2011, there are 13 complaints filed. The decrease, in my opinion, could be a result of fear of reprisal or more effort from management addressing concerns in the resolution period. The increase later could be a result of ruling by fear and individuals beginning to stand up for their rights more because of the challenging society and need to be treated fairly.

## Number of Complaints by Bases

| Complaints by Basis Sec. 1614.704 (d) | | | Comparative Data (Sec. 1614.705) | | | | | | | 2011 thru 06/30/11 | | |
|---|---|---|---|---|---|---|---|---|---|---|---|---|
| | | | Previous Fiscal Year Data | | | | | | | | | |
| Note: Complaints can be filed alleging multiple bases. The sum of the bases may not equal total complaints filed. | | | '02 | '03 | '04 | '05 | '06 | '07 | '08 | '09 | '10 | '11 |
| Race | | | 19 | 12 | 13 | 11 | 7 | 6 | 24 | 12 | 13 | 3 |
| Reprisal | 24 | 24 | 23 | 14 | 12 | 21 | 20 | 21 | 20 | | | 4 |
| Sex | 17 | 16 | 13 | 7 | 3 | 11 | 20 | 16 | 10 | | | 10 |

This depicts that complaints based on **race** started out in 2002 at 19 for EEOC and decreased over the years until 2008 where they were heightened to 24. In 2011 there are only 3 reported 06/30/11 according to the information I reviewed on the site. In **Reprisal** cases for prior EEO activity, complaints started off high at 24 and though decreased maintained a concerning level, in my opinion from 2007 to 2010. In 2011 there were 4 reported. This could be based on ruling by fear and management control. However, some managers and organizations are implementing more conflict management programs, early intervention and effective communication training programs. There are several reasons for increases and decreases in complaints filed and why they are filed.

You should always be aware of the difference between individual and class complaints. A class of employees can file what is known as a class action complaint. The difference between an individual and class complaint is that a class has to be of the same protected category, i.e., same race, sex, disability, etc. There must be numerosity, commonality and an agent of the class. A few people would not constitute a class. It has been indicated that a number such as 40 or more could meet that threshold; however, EEOC can accept a class action with less if it is deemed to meet the basic definition of a class being affected. At some level of the process, the class should have an attorney in order for its continuous processing. These types of cases can stifle an organization. Usually trust is compromised, operations are affected, and there can be a great lack of morale.

## SELLOUTS

What is a sellout? Is it the person who will not testify on your behalf? Is it the person that sucks up to management and demonstrates a "yes sir mista boss" mentality in order to get ahead, or is it the person that will lie and throw you under the bus in order to advance in the organization? During my career, I have seen each of these types of individuals. In one instance, I was aware of a supervisor forced to discipline an employee/complainant because they challenged their unfair treatment. The supervisor actually told me that his office was doing what they were told, but they would not testify to that. The supervisor empathized with the individual but had to follow leadership's direction. During informal counseling, I had to somehow expose the motivation by getting everyone together and asking specific questions about decisions that were made based on documented presentations. It is difficult for an individual to maintain that they had nothing to do with a decision when their signature appears on the document. On the other side of that coin, a case that involved a complainant who truly believed that their peers and supervisor (of the same race) were sellouts because they did not condone the complainant's absent without leave practices. This demonstrated that a perception may not always be accurate.

How can civil rights survive when the very ones who should represent the truth are the ones who are trying to exclude so they can be promoted or for other reasons that are beyond me? I am aware of a situation wherein an employee actually made false accusations to management about a minority leader that had been supportive and was, in fact, responsible for the career growth of that same employee. An Administrative Board of Investigation (ABOI) was implemented and the environment became very distrustful. The employee was supported by being moved to the management's office because there was a possibility of retaliation. The leader was left without resources but was still required to complete the task. The investigation did not prevail but, nevertheless, it is amazing the number of ABOI's that take place in which management looks for reasons to cause harm. They can exonerate as well. The way in which the ABOI's are conducted is unreal. Usually the Agency Head appoints the investigating staff. Then, at the completion of the investigation, the Agency retains the report even after a request under the Freedom of Information Act is submitted. In the name of privacy of others, it is most likely a long time before an individual knows who said what, although the individual investigated has limited privacy rights during that process. Something needs to be done to develop a more fair administrative process or additional training for all employees, not just those who become Administrative Investigators.

It is common for people to sell out others. But sometimes we may believe we have been sold out when, in fact, we have not taken care of our own business and made certain that our grass is green. Avoid situations and the truth will hopefully speak for itself. In the current world, we still have those who are afraid to testify on behalf of others when the truth can resolve matters. If leaders are true to their integrity, they can recognize sellouts and those who have the courage to just tell the truth. In my years, I've noticed that organizations with employees who are free to express their thoughts without fear of retaliation have a more satisfied workforce that comes to work happier and is more productive.

## THE COURAGE TO EFFECT CHANGE

First and foremost, know your rights. Be diligent and prudent in learning and understanding what you can and cannot do, as well as what others can and cannot do to you. Be aware that you cannot be treated differently because of your race, color, national origin, disability, age, parental status, genetic information, sex gender, sexual orientation and other issues. There are several regulations, laws and Executive Orders in place to protect you. Are you familiar with Title VII of the Civil Rights Act of 1964? This law came into existence as a result of the civil rights struggles and the marches lead by those who had the courage to effect change. What about the Equal Pay Act? Women should be paid the same salary for doing the same type of work as men. Some are unaware of pregnancy laws. Pregnant women have the right not to be treated as less than and the right to have a certain length of time off to deliver and return to work. Know your timelines. In the Federal government, the timelines are different than in the state or private sectors, not to mention city and county governments. You only have 45 days to contact an EEO Counselor for discrimination in Federal but, in state, you have about 10 months. There is the Department of Fair Employment and Housing that handles private sector cases.

Understand that an EEO Counselor is not your representative. Their role is to attempt to resolve matters at the lowest level possible, fact find and then report on their inquiry. You then have a right to file a formal complaint at the end of the informal stage. You should always be willing to come to the table to negotiate during mediation toward resolution. The only time you should not consider this is when there are some serious issues such as sexual harassment that is severe, criminal intent, or some illegal actions such as assault involved. At the formal level, you should receive an investigation that is timely. Know your time frames because at some point, if the investigation is not completed (180 days in Federal after formal filing), you can request a hearing by an Administrative Judge from the Equal Employment Opportunity Commission. Of course, there are appeals at that level that include filing a civil action in court. Don't think that you know everything, but know your rights and also behave at work in a professional and appropriate manner at all times. Your reputation precedes you. You have some responsibility for others' perception of you. Just when you think you are out of the woods, things can happen.

In terms of filing timelines, the Equal Employment Opportunity Commission provides a general explanation via their website. Note the following information:

## Time Limits For Filing A Charge

The anti-discrimination laws give you a limited amount of time to file a charge of discrimination. In general, you need to file a charge within 180 calendar days from the day the discrimination took place. The 180 calendar day filing deadline is extended to 300 calendar days if a state or local agency enforces a law that prohibits employment discrimination on the same basis. The rules are slightly different for age discrimination charges. For age discrimination, the filing deadline is only extended to 300 days if there is a state law prohibiting age discrimination in employment and a state agency or authority enforcing that law. The deadline is not extended if only a local law prohibits age discrimination.

*Note*: Federal employees and job applicants have a different complaint process, and generally must contact an agency EEO

Counselor within 45 days. The time limit can be extended under certain circumstances.

Regardless of how much time you have to file, it is best to file as soon as you have decided that is what you would like to do.

Time limits for filing a charge with EEOC generally will not be extended while you attempt to resolve a dispute through another forum such as an internal grievance procedure, a union grievance, arbitration or mediation before filing a charge with EEOC. Other forums for resolution may be pursued at the same time as the processing of the EEOC charge.

Holidays and weekends are included in the calculation, although if the deadline falls on a weekend or holiday, you will have until the next business day. Calculating how much time you have to file a charge is complicated. If you aren't sure how much time is left, you should contact one of the field offices as soon as possible so they can assess whether or not you still have time.

## If More Than One Discriminatory Event Took Place

Also, if more than one discriminatory event took place, the deadline usually applies to each event. For example, let's say you were demoted and then fired a year later. You believe the employer based its decision to demote and fire you on your race, and you file a charge the day after your discharge. In this case, only your claim of discriminatory discharge is timely. In other words, you must have filed a charge challenging the demotion within 180/300 days from the day you were demoted. If you didn't, only your discharge would be investigated. There is one exception to this general rule and that is if you are alleging ongoing harassment.

## Ongoing Harassment

In harassment cases, you must file your charge within 180 or 300 days of the last incident of harassment, although we will look at all incidents of harassment when investigating your charge, even if the earlier incidents happened more than 180/300 days earlier.

## Equal Pay Act And Time Limits

If you plan to file a charge alleging a violation of the Equal Pay Act (which prohibits sex discrimination in wages and benefits), different deadlines apply. Under the Equal Pay Act, you don't need to file a charge of discrimination with EEOC. Instead, you are allowed to go directly to court and file a lawsuit. The deadline for filing a charge or lawsuit under the EPA is two years from the day you received the last discriminatory paycheck (this is extended to three years in the case of willful discrimination).

## Equal Pay Act And Title VII And Time Limits

Keep in mind, Title VII also makes it illegal to discriminate based on sex in the payment of wages and benefits. What this means is, if you have an Equal Pay Act claim, you may also want to file a Title VII claim. In order to pursue a Title VII claim, you must file a charge with EEOC first. Filing a Title VII charge will not extend the deadline for filing an EPA lawsuit. Figuring out how much time you have to file a charge is complicated. It also can be difficult to figure out the pros and cons of filing a charge under the EPA instead of a lawsuit. Members of a field office staff would be happy to speak with you to explore your options.

In January of 2010, I retired as an Equal Employment Opportunity Program Manager, having served for 30 years in that area of expertise. My retirement was not necessarily planned for that time, but was encouraged based on what I had experienced in the days and months prior to that date. I believed myself to be a neutral party when it came to people's civil rights in the workplace. I held all accountable for their actions, perceptions and behavior when it came to equity. One of my leaders mentioned to me that, for several years, I had basically made the organization adhere to the promotion of diversity. This particular organization, he said, was known as a white hospital. With my strong and positive attitude about fairness, it did not even phase me because I understood what my job was and what I would do to do it right. I challenged management when they were wrong about actions that appeared to be discriminatory, whether based on race, religion, sex, color, disabilities, age, natural origin, parental status, genetics or reprisal (retaliation). Some organizations control their EEO Managers to protect them from liability when they discriminate. I was not the one. The environment had grown to be in conflict with the powers that be, so an effort to separate me was launched. Fabrications were established and there was an attack on my integrity, my fitness for duty and my core value to the organization. I had been asked about my retirement plans on several occasions, prior to the point at which an administrative board of investigation against me was discreetly assembled. I had no problem with that because I did not want to work for an organization that did not see the value of what I brought to the table. Many colleagues and acquaintances knew me as a dynamic EEO representative, both in and out of the organization I worked. I had a clear case of discrimination and reprisal but I chose to let go and retire by turning a cheek and walking in God's light. Today I am fine. Race was not the only issue; I have a visual impairment. Although some accommodations were made (largely because they had to be, particularly for someone in my position of EEO). That was also held against me. I realized that all of the employees, managers and supervisors as well as organizations with which I interacted were helped fairly. I gave my career to the service of others. Sometimes that can be risky, but my conscious is very clear and God has my back on every turn.

Writing this book will hopefully open eyes and ignite courage to stand up for what is right. "We the People" is more than just a phrase. "We the People" must expect, command and demand adherence to our rights. Leaders must have the vision and courage to support and practice fair treatment in numbers and not for just a few. Are civil rights on life support? Yes, it is. You could not imagine what many organizations are doing with this notion of having civil rights in the workplace. There should be no such thing as an At Will employment agreement or state of affairs. What are our politicians thinking by allowing organizations to abuse their power by condoning and practicing discriminatory activities? I am not talking about frivolous complaining but actual blatant discrimination.

While conducting my private business, "Distinguished Consultant Corporation", in which I represent, mediate, train, review, implement and present, I've found that there are several organizations that are not afraid to discriminate. Their leadership has a mentality of "we can do whatever we want to our employees" and therefore, they do not respect individuals' civil rights. Are civil rights on life support? I was amazed to find that in some cases, employees did not know where to go to complain or who to contact if they were being mistreated. Of course, all organizations are not like that and some are better than others, but there should be no flexibility in the way that good employees are treated. There would be no organization and no one to supervise without those subordinates that hold the companies together.

A society, organization, leader or employee that looks at themselves are healthy. Those who deny their own shortcomings or evil breed despair. People will pay for power, even if it is at the expense of those they oppress. Where are we in today's world? Time demands change, whether it is for the good or bad. Do we have the courage to affect change? Let's look in the mirror as a people.

In this anniversary year of celebrating the legacy of Dr. Martin Luther King, Jr., Andrew Krzmarzuick wrote a very thought provoking article entitled "Are We Beyond Race in the Workplace"

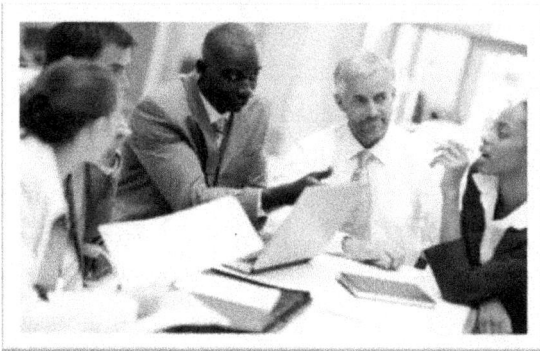

He stated that "As we celebrate the legacy of Dr. Martin Luther King, Jr. on Monday, I wanted to ask some tough questions. Here we are - almost half a century after the signature Civil Rights legislation of 1968 - and I'm wondering:"

1 - Are we 'beyond race' in today's workplace?

2 - Do our interactions appear to be "color blind" or is there still an awkwardness and uncertainty that seems to simmer just under the surface?

3 - Is there more that needs to happen to create equity and cross-cultural understanding? How does your organization address diversity?"

A couple of the responses were very interesting that he shared with his reading audience. Some replies to his discussion questions are the following:

## Replies to This Discussion

Reply 1 - I like to think we are, and I hope that it isn't just in the workplace that we are able to move beyond things like race, religion, age, sex, etc. In my opinion this is one area where social media/networking plays a big role. When we interact online, whether it is through Twitter, FB, or in virtual worlds, many times we don't really know who is behind the words or avatar we see. For the first time, these tools allow us to communicate without any awareness of any other aspect of a person other than their words and thoughts. So perhaps by interacting in this way we are re-training ourselves to realize all that other stuff should not be influencing our interactions in a negative manner.

However, as a genealogist, I do want to add that I in no way think we should be "blind" to race and culture as others sometimes suggest. Our ancestry and cultural background brought us to where we are today and helps make us who we are so understanding and celebrating everyone's heritage is very important.

Perhaps that is where it becomes sensitive; in acknowledging and honoring someone's heritage, we might have to treat someone a little differently to avoid offending their beliefs. But maybe this is no different than just being considerate of others in general - if we care about someone and know that something bothers them, for whatever reason, we try to avoid doing it.

Reply 2 - Tough question. I think it's too much to ever expect to be 100% beyond race. Just like we won't ever be beyond gender.

Most organizations I've worked in have diversity training as well as recognize various months (Black History Month, Hispanic Heritage Month).

Luckily the government is one of the most diverse working places in the U.S. (and military is #1). I think the effort in recruiting all races has paid off as for many racial groups the government is seen as a "great job" that will treat you well regardless of race.

Reply 3 - I'm almost afraid to answer, but let's break the ice as it does no good to be silent.

Since this is not a "historical" but "current" question, it seems that race & gender are still an issue. Let's focus on race. Since this question is asked today, Martin Luther King Day, may give the impression "today it's safe to have a discussion."

A department can still be judged as "balanced" or "unbalanced" as far as race participation at all levels. Hearing comments like "I've been over here (in America) for only two weeks and half the office seems tense around me for what happened 200 years ago in your history" What was interesting, *really* interesting is how I did not feel any difference in tension between any group or race. Hence my fear of answering - what is out there that I do not know. Does not race add to the experience? If so why?

I applaud Andrew for the courage to discuss the issues and ask the questions that need answers, understanding that change begins with a conversation. Those leaders or organizations that are willing to have the discussion should be the leaders of today and tomorrow. We must have the courage to affect change.

## ACCOUNTABILITY

As a civil rights consultant, I learned that there are strongholds in place within a broken system that those who have a perception of power are not willing to adjust. Civil rights are on life support because of a lack of accountability. In my 30 years and, most notably, today, I see how accountability must start at the top of the mountain and roll down like a flood of righteousness, cleansing all that is in its path. Those whom we elect to serve the community should have a true sense of fairness and great expectations for equity with no tolerance for anything less. We should research before we push that button at the voter's booth. Those individuals should hold all under their jurisdictions accountable to the same degree.

We should break down these strongholds that have established unchallenged protocols to instill fear because they have the luxury of using taxpayers' dollars to discriminate against the taxpayer who cannot afford an expensive attorney. Managers and leaders or organizations that do not hesitate to discriminate should be sanctioned more severely. For example, take the money out of their paychecks. If multiple complaints are filed at a particular organization or against a particular leader, more than likely, something is going on. Organizations should pull their resources together to help provide support.

I am a member of an organization entitled Blacks in Government (BIG). BIG is a non-profit 501©3 organization that promotes professional development, equity and excellence. Its objectives include eliminating racism, promoting ethnic pride, networking and advocating for Blacks and African Americans as well as others in the community. The latter includes training and education for

45

all, in particular, mentoring our youth. It was founded in 1975 and chartered in 1976 in Washington, DC. It is amazing how many people I meet that have not heard of this noteworthy organization. An informational website of www.bignet.org gives access to all it is about.

More organizations and civil rights champions should work together.

Our power is in the numbers and resources available to us. Those who can should take cases pro bono to help the needy. It is those who have unhealthy power that can create unhealthy environments, so most people or employees do not want the hassle. It is time for change.

Performance Ratings for leaders should include specific statements on their ability to promote diversity, maintain an equitable workplace with minimal complaints, awards for special programs that demonstrate a commitment to a discriminatory free work environment and other specific statements that are not generic but realistic and achievable. An investigation of the way in which Human Resources offices are managed in regard to its resources, the employees, should be conducted in every organization by a carefully selected group of objective experts to see if power is healthy or unhealthy in that area. Equal Employment Opportunity Managers should be supported in their goals to assure that all are treated fairly and held accountable. Conversations and open discussions with unions should be revisited, with notes made of those unions who are sleeping with the enemy. Those who challenge appropriately should be respected. How do we hold accountability is the major question?

It is clear that the Equal Employment Opportunity Commission is the enforcer of civil rights laws. There is such a backlog of cases that some judges or investigators are overwhelmed; time lines may prevent them from addressing the issues as effectively as they could. If there is such a backlog of cases, then something is wrong in the organizations. We must hire more people and support them in their efforts to hold agencies accountable. Most people I talk to would rather have their case take a little longer to resolve than to have a rushed judgment of no discrimination when they know the behavior took place. Some agencies do not even have training on EEO or sexual harassment unless a major case surfaces, giving them unwanted visibility. If EEOC applies appropriate and strong sanctions against organizations that will affect the wrong doer in a significant way, we would have greater sensitivity to employees and less control. A psychological exam should be given to all leaders to see how they fare in respect to the treatment of people of all backgrounds. Then we may not have so many complaints.

Being discriminated against is almost the same as being hung from a tree and tarred and feathered or receiving thirty lashes, especially when you do not know how you are going to feed your children, achieve that promotion to help pay the mortgage or come to work without stress or fear of not being accepted because you have a disability. Are civil rights on life support? They are when no one wants to step up and say, "yes, I heard the supervisor make that comment or a racial remark" without fear of retaliation.

The appropriate leaders such as our politicians, EEOC, the Human Rights Commission, Unions and Administrators as well as we the people should introduce a process into the workplace whereby parties in a dispute can be ordered to or volunteer to participate in polygraph test to find the truth before unnecessary cost, wasted time and disrupted operations occur. There would be a much smaller number of complaints or backlog, cases will be resolved during mediations and most importantly, leaders will ensure they are doing the right thing. Imagine that.

One of the greatest resources of an organization is its willingness to come to the table and discuss or listen to an aggrieved person's perspective. There are Alternative Dispute Resolution methods that could help. For example, Mediation, Conciliation, Arbitration and Group Facilitation are available for use. The most popular forum utilized is Mediation, a process involving a third party helping the two parties arrive at an equitable conclusion to resolve their concerns. The process should work toward a win-win situation and not necessarily toward compromise. The overall goal is arriving at a third alternative that neither party may not have reached by themselves. Unless there are extenuating circumstances, both parties should always be willing to communicate. This tool should be utilized by Management and Employees alike. Holding all accountable for resolution efforts is extremely important.

Let's look at a few relevant case studies. I hope you find this interesting and educational. People think that having power is all that is needed while most of the time, it is perceived power that one believes that he or she has. Then there is what others perceive that someone has. Perceived power can be whisked away as soon as it is perceived. However, having knowledge and awareness has its own power, sense of stability and respect. Take a look at the following information provided from the EEOC website:

CASE STUDY No. 1

Sukeena Stephens,
Complainant,

v.

Janet Napolitano,
Secretary,
Department of Homeland Security,
Agency.
Appeal No. 0120083445
Hearing No. 160-2005-00053X
Agency No. TSAF-03-2639

DECISION

On July 30, 2008, complainant filed an appeal from the agency's June 24,2008 final decision concerning her equal employment opportunity (EEO)Complaint alleging employment discrimination in violation of Title VII of the Civil Rights Act of 1964 (Title VII), as amended, 42 U.S.C. § 2000e et seq. and Section 501 of the Rehabilitation Act of 1973 (Rehabilitation Act), as amended, 29 U.S.C. § 791 et seq. The appeal is deemed timely and is accepted pursuant to 29 C.F.R. § 1614.405(a). For the following reasons, the Commission AFFIRMS the agency's final order.

At the time of events giving rise to this complaint, complainant worked as a Federal Air Marshall at the agency's New York Field Office. In a formal EEO complaint dated December 9, 2003, complaint alleged that she was discriminated against on the bases of race (African-American), sex (female) and disability (uterine tumors) when, since Summer 2002, the agency denied her requests to transfer to its Washington Field Office.

After more than 180 days passed following the filing of her formal complaint, on July 22, 2004, complainant requested a hearing before an EEOC Administrative Judge (AJ). At the hearing stage, in a decision dated October 3, 2006, the AJ noted that the agency took 764 days from when Complainant filed her formal complaint to complete its investigation, and found that such delay ultimately disadvantaged complainant in a determination as to discrimination and the agency was on notice that sanctions could apply. The AJ stated, hence, he found it appropriate to impose the sanction of a decision fully in favor of complainant as to race and age, but not disability, when the agency denied her request to transfer from the agency's New York Field Office to its Washington Field Office. The AJ found that complainant established an Inference of discrimination based on race and sex sufficient to support a default judgment in her favor. As relief, the AJ ordered the agency to reassign complainant to the Washington Field Office, award compensatory damages, attorney's fees and costs, and post a notice of a finding of discrimination. With regard to compensatory damages and attorney's fees, the AJ instructed complainant to provide evidence supporting such an award to him and the agency within thirty calendar days from receipt of his decision. The AJ stated that failure to do so "shall be deemed a waiver of attorney's fees, costs and compensatory damages."

In a decision dated January 18, 2008, the AJ found that complainant "effectively waived her compensatory damages and attorney's fees/costs in the[e instant] complaint." The AJ stated that the complainant remains entitled to reassignment to the agency's Washington Field Office and the posting of a notice of discrimination. On June 24, 2008, the agency issued a final decision implementing the AJ's decision. The instant appeal from complainant followed.

On appeal, complainant stated that the AJ abused his discretion by informing her legal representative that he would set up mediation on the matter and failing to do so. Complainant stated that, between November 2006 and July 2007, she was in consistent contact with the AJ and agency regarding mediation of the matter through a peer of the assigned EEOC AJ and that, on July 30, 2007, she timely filed a response to the agency's motion to dismiss. Complainant stated that the AJ's assertion that she did not respond to the agency's motion and sought to abandon her claim is incorrect. On appeal, complainant stated that the AJ did not give her appropriate notice of such a severe action and, if he had, she would have submitted her request for remedy. In opposition to complainant's appeal, the agency stated that, after numerous extensions, complainant failed to follow the AJ's order of submitting evidence in support of compensatory damages and attorney's fees. The agency noted that complainant had ample opportunity to submit her evidence as she was given an extension date of March 2, 2007 and failed to respond to the agency's July 2007 motion to dismiss.

Here, the sole issue before the Commission is complainant's entitlement to compensatory damages and attorney's fees and costs following an agency-implemented AJ finding of discrimination based on race and sex. To calculate appropriate relief, an AJ may require a complainant to produce evidence demonstrating entitlement and may, in his/her discretion, find a claim waived if a complainant fails to produce such evidence.

See EEOC Management Directive 110, Ch. 7, Sec. III.D.11-13, 7-12 & 7-13 (November 9, 1999). Such is the case here. The record reveals that the AJ instructed complainant to, within 30 days of receipt of the decision, submit evidence for calculating damages and attorney's fees. Complainant sought mediation regarding such calculations, but more than seven months after the AJ's interim decision, mediation still was not scheduled or received. The record is unclear as to why complainant continued to seek this option, rather than or in addition to submitting her relief evidence and the agency inquired about her evidence. We find the AJ's finding of waiver of compensatory damages and attorney's fees appropriate. Hence, we AFFIRM the final agency decision.

STATEMENT OF RIGHTS - ON APPEAL

RECONSIDERATION (M1208)

The Commission may, in its discretion, reconsider the decision in this case if the complainant or the agency submits a written request containing arguments or evidence which tend to establish that:

1. The appellate decision involved a clearly erroneous interpretation of material fact or law; or
2. The appellate decision will have a substantial impact on the policies, practices, or operations of the agency.

Requests to reconsider, with supporting statement or brief, must be filed with the Office of Federal Operations (OFO) within thirty (30) calendar days of receipt of this decision or within twenty (20) calendar days of receipt of another party's timely request for reconsideration. See 29 C.F.R. § 1614.405; Equal Employment Opportunity Management Directive for 29 C.F.R. Part 1614 (EEO MD-110), 9-18 (November 9, 1999). All requests and arguments must be submitted to the Director, Office of Federal Operations, Equal Employment Opportunity Commission, P.O.

Box 77960, Washington, DC 20013. In the absence of a legible postmark, the request to reconsider shall be deemed timely filed if it is received by mail within five days of the expiration of the applicable filing period.

See 29 C.F.R. § 1614.604. The request or opposition must also include proof of service on the other party. Failure to file within the time period will result in dismissal of your request for reconsideration as untimely, unless extenuating circumstances prevented the timely filing of the request. Any supporting documentation must be submitted with your request for reconsideration. The Commission will consider requests for reconsideration filed after the deadline only in very limited circumstances. See 29 C.F.R. § 1614.604(c).

COMPLAINANT'S RIGHT TO FILE A CIVIL ACTION (S0408)

You have the right to file a civil action in an appropriate United States District Court within ninety (90) calendar days from the date that you receive this decision. If you file a civil action, you must name as the defendant in the complaint the person who is the official agency head or department head, identifying that person by his or her full name and official title. Failure to do so may result in the dismissal of your case in court. "Agency" or "department" means the national organization, and not the local office, facility or department in which you work. If you file a request to reconsider and also file a civil action, filing a civil action will terminate the administrative processing of your complaint.

## RIGHT TO REQUEST COUNSEL (Z1008)

If you decide to file a civil action, and if you do not have or cannot afford the services of an attorney, you may request from the Court that the Court appoint an attorney to represent you and that the Court also permit you to file the action without payment of fees, costs, or other security. See Title VII of the Civil Rights Act of 1964, as amended, 42 U.S.C. § 2000e et seq.; the Rehabilitation Act of 1973, as amended, 29 U.S.C. §§ 791, 794(c). The grant or denial of the request is within the sole discretion of the Court. Filing a request for an attorney with the Court does not extend your time in which to file a civil action. Both the request and the civil action must be filed within the time limits as stated in the paragraph above ("Right to File A Civil Action").

---

## CASE STUDY No. 2

Mohamed Hewady v. Department of Agriculture
01A42841
11/4/04
Mohamed Hewady,
Complainant,
v.
Ann M. Veneman,
Secretary,
Department of Agriculture,
Agency.
Appeal No. 01A42841
Agency No. 020814

DECISION

Complainant timely initiated an appeal from a final agency decision (FAD) concerning his complaint of unlawful employment discrimination in violation of Title VII of the Civil Rights Act of 1964 (Title VII), as amended, 42 U.S.C. § 2000e et seq. and Section 501 of the Rehabilitation Act of 1973 (Rehabilitation Act), as amended, 29 U.S.C. § 791 et seq. The appeal is accepted pursuant to 29 C.F.R. § 1614.405. For the following reasons, the Commission AFFIRMS the agency's final decision.

The record reveals that during the relevant time, complainant was employed as a Plant Protection and Quarantine ("PPQ") Officer at the agency's Newark, New Jersey facility. Complainant sought EEO counseling and subsequently filed a formal complaint on September 17, 2002, alleging that he was discriminated against on the bases of national origin (Muslim), religion (Muslim), and disability (diabetes) when: he was not allowed to repeat the New Officer Training, which resulted in his termination from the program on July 1, 2002; and he was not provided an accommodation of his disability while attending PPQ Officer training.

At the conclusion of the investigation, complainant was informed of his right to request a hearing before an EEOC Administrative Judge or alternatively, to receive a final decision by the agency. When complainant failed to respond within the time period specified in 29 C.F.R. § 1614.108(f), the agency issued a final decision.

In its FAD, the agency concluded that complainant established a prima facie case of religious discrimination. However, the agency found that it articulated a legitimate, non-discriminatory reason for complainant's termination from the New Officer Training Program; namely, that he failed to achieve a passing score of 80% on his first three tests in the training. In accordance with the rules at the time, complainant was not permitted to re-take the test.

Although complainant presented evidence that others failed, but were permitted to stay in the New Officer Training course, the agency found that they were not similarly situated to complainant. In that regard, the agency noted that due to an EEO complaint filed over the potential disparate impact of the New Officer Training requirements on an unnamed protected group, the agency decided to suspend the automatic termination. When the Office of Personnel Management conducted a study and concluded that the test did not result in a disparate impact, the agency reinstated its requirements. Accordingly, those who entered on duty during the suspended period of September 2001 through May 2002, were not subjected to the same rules as complainant. The record revealed that the comparatives cited by complainant were included in this class of people, and complainant was not.

As for his claim that he was denied reasonable accommodation, the agency found that complainant requested a hot plate and refrigerator in his hotel room, and access to an exercise room while he attended New Officer Training. However, he failed to establish a prima facie case of disability discrimination because he failed to identify how his diabetes substantially limited a major life activity.

Complainant makes no arguments on appeal.

Although the Commission finds that complainant properly established a prima facie case of religious discrimination, we also find that complainant failed to present evidence that more likely than not, the agency's articulated reasons for its actions were a pretext for discrimination. In reaching this conclusion, we note that complainant presented no evidence whatsoever that would contradict the agency's reasons for its actions. Furthermore, complainant did not argue that the New Officer Training requirements caused any disparate impact on him because of his membership in any protected group.<1> Finally, we find no evidence of a discriminatory motive when he was terminated from his position.<2> As for complainant's reasonable accommodation claim, we find that assuming, arguendo, that complainant is an individual with a disability, we find he failed to prove the agency denied him a reasonable accommodation for his diabetes. Complainant requested that the agency provide him with a hot plate, refrigerator and that he had access to an exercise room while he was out of town for the New Officer Training.

The record reveals that complainant was provided with a room with a microwave, refrigerator, and had access to another hotel which had an exercise room, which was within walking distance from his hotel.

We find that this was a reasonable accommodation of complainant's alleged disability. In so finding, we note that complainant did not specify how the agency's accommodation did not satisfy his medical needs, such as with respect to his food preparation or exercise needs.

Therefore, after a careful review of the record, including arguments and evidence not specifically addressed in this decision, we affirm the FAD.

STATEMENT OF RIGHTS - ON APPEAL

RECONSIDERATION (M0701)

The Commission may, in its discretion, reconsider the decision in this case if the complainant or the agency submits a written request containing arguments or evidence which tend to establish that:

1. The appellate decision involved a clearly erroneous interpretation of material fact or law; or

2. The appellate decision will have a substantial impact on the policies, practices, or operations of the agency.

Requests to reconsider, with supporting statement or brief, must be filed with the Office of Federal Operations (OFO) within thirty (30) calendar days of receipt of this decision or within twenty (20) calendar days of receipt of another party's timely request for reconsideration.

See 29 C.F.R. § 1614.405; Equal Employment Opportunity Management Directive for 29 C.F.R. Part 1614 (EEO MD-110), 9-18 (November 9, 1999). All requests and arguments must be submitted to the Director, Office of Federal Operations, Equal Employment Opportunity Commission, P.O. Box 19848, Washington, D.C. 20036. In the absence of a legible postmark, the request to reconsider shall be deemed timely filed if it is received by mail within five days of the expiration of the applicable filing period.

See 29 C.F.R. § 1614.604. The request or opposition must also include proof of service on the other party.

Failure to file within the time period will result in dismissal of your request for reconsideration as untimely, unless extenuating circumstances prevented the timely filing of the request. Any supporting documentation must be submitted with your request for reconsideration. The Commission will consider requests for reconsideration filed after the deadline only in very limited circumstances. See 29 C.F.R. § 1614.604(c).

COMPLAINANT'S RIGHT TO FILE A CIVIL ACTION (S0900)

You have the right to file a civil action in an appropriate United States District Court within ninety (90) calendar days from the date that you receive this decision. If you file a civil action, you must name as the defendant in the complaint the person who is the official agency head or department head, identifying that person by his or her full name and official title. Failure to do so may result in the dismissal of your case in court. "Agency" or "department" means the national organization, and not the local office, facility or department in which you work. If you file a request to reconsider and also file a civil action, filing a civil action will terminate the administrative processing of your complaint.

RIGHT TO REQUEST COUNSEL (Z1199)

If you decide to file a civil action, and if you do not have or cannot afford the services of an attorney, you may request that the Court appoint an attorney to represent you and that the Court permit you to file the action without payment of fees, costs, or other security. See Title VII of the Civil Rights Act of 1964, as amended, 42 U.S.C. § 2000e et seq. ;the Rehabilitation Act of 1973, as amended, 29 U.S.C. §§ 791, 794(c).

The grant or denial of the request is within the sole discretion of the Court. Filing a request for an attorney does not extend your time in which to file a civil action. Both the request and the civil action must be filed within the time limits as stated in the paragraph above ("Right to File A Civil Action").

CASE STUDY No. 3

Pamela G. Marshall v. Department of the Army
03A60026
December 16, 2005
Pamela G. Marshall,
Petitioner,
v.
Dr. Francis J. Harvey,
Secretary,
Department of the Army,
Agency.
Petition No. 03A60026
MSPB No. DC-0752-05-0221-I-1
DECISION

Petitioner filed a timely petition with the Equal Employment Opportunity Commission asking for review of a Final Order issued by the Merit Systems Protection Board (MSPB) concerning her claim of discrimination in violation of Title VII of the Civil Rights Act of 1964 (Title VII), as amended, 42 U.S.C. § 2000e et seq.

Petitioner, a Secretary at the agency's Human Resources Command in Alexandria, Virginia, alleged that she was discriminated against on the basis of sex (female) when she was subjected to sexual harassment and removed from her position. Specifically, petitioner alleged her supervisor used inappropriate language around her. The record shows that petitioner was removed from her position for being absent without leave on several occasions. In addition, the record shows that she had previously been disciplined for attendance problems. When petitioner withdrew her request for a hearing, the MSPB Administrative Judge (AJ) issued a decision finding that petitioner was unable to support her claims of sexual harassment or sex discrimination. Petitioner sought review by the full Board, which denied her petition. Petitioner then filed her petition for review with the Commission, for the first time arguing that she was discriminated against based on her sexual orientation and her status as a parent. The Commission notes that it has no jurisdiction over discrimination based on sexual orientation. Petitioner's status as a parent apparently is related to her Family Medical Leave Act claims over which the Commission also has no jurisdiction.

EEOC Regulations provide that the Commission has jurisdiction over mixed case appeals on which the MSPB has issued a decision that makes determinations on allegations of discrimination. 29 C.F.R. § 1614.303 et seq. The Commission must determine whether the decision of the MSPB with respect to the allegation of discrimination constitutes a correct interpretation of any applicable law, rule, regulation or policy directive, and is supported by the evidence in the record as a whole.

29 C.F.R. § 1614.305(c).

Based upon a thorough review of the record and for the foregoing reasons, it is the decision of the Commission to concur with the final decision of the MSPB finding no discrimination. The Commission finds that the MSPB's decision constitutes a correct interpretation of the laws, rules, regulations, and policies governing this matter and is supported by the evidence in the record as a whole.

PETITIONER'S RIGHT TO FILE A CIVIL ACTION (W0900)

This decision of the Commission is final, and there is no further right of administrative appeal from the Commission's decision. You have the right to file a civil action in an appropriate United States District Court, based on the decision of the Merit Systems Protection Board, within thirty (30) calendar days of the date that you receive this decision.

If you file a civil action, you must name as the defendant in the complaint the person who is the official agency head or department head, identifying that person by his or her full name and official title.

Failure to do so may result in the dismissal of your case in court. "Agency" or "department" means the national organization, and not the local office, facility or department in which you work.

RIGHT TO REQUEST COUNSEL (Z1199)

If you decide to file a civil action, and if you do not have or cannot afford the services of an attorney, you may request that the Court appoint an attorney to represent you and that the Court permit you to file the action without payment of fees, costs, or other security. See Title VII of the Civil Rights Act of 1964, as amended, 42 U.S.C. § 2000e et seq.; the Rehabilitation Act of 1973, as amended, 29 U.S.C. §§ 791, 794(c). The grant or denial of the request is within the sole discretion of the Court. Filing a request for an attorney does not extend your time in which to file a civil action. Both the request and the civil action must be filed within the time limits as stated in the paragraph above ("Right to File A Civil Action").

---

## CASE STUDY No. 4

Ollie Smith,
Complainant,
v.
John E. Potter,
Postmaster General,
United States Postal Service,
(Great Lakes Area),
Agency.
Appeal No. 0120073064
Hearing No. 443-07-00063X
Agency No. 1J-531-0111-06

DECISION

On June 25, 2007, complainant filed an appeal from the agency's June 6, 2007 final decision concerning her equal employment opportunity (EEO) complaint alleging employment discrimination in violation of the Age Discrimination in Employment Act of 1967 (ADEA), as amended, 29 U.S.C. § 621 et seq. The appeal is deemed timely and is accepted pursuant to 29 C.F.R. § 1614.405(a). For the following reasons, the Commission AFFIRMS the agency's final decision.

ISSUE PRESENTED

Whether the agency properly found that complainant was not subjected to discrimination based on age when she was terminated.

BACKGROUND

At the time of the events giving rise to this complaint, complainant worked as a Casual Mail Handler at an agency's facility in Oak Creek, Wisconsin. The record reflects that on August 12, 2006, complainant's supervisor, the Supervisor, Distribution Operations (SDO), instructed her to work overtime after her tour had ended. Complainant did not work overtime as directed, and she left the premises without permission.

On August 13, 2006, complainant was terminated for failure to follow instructions. In November 2006, complainant filed an EEO complaint alleging that she was discriminated against on the basis of age (53 years old at the time of the alleged incident) when, on August 13, 2006, she was terminated.

At the conclusion of the investigation, complainant was provided with a copy of the report of investigation and a notice of her right to request a hearing before an EEOC Administrative Judge (AJ). Complainant timely requested a hearing but subsequently withdrew her request. Consequently, the agency issued a final decision pursuant to 29 C.F.R. § 1614.110(b). The decision concluded that complainant failed to prove that she was subjected to age discrimination as alleged. Specifically, the agency's decision found that complainant failed to establish a prima facie case of age discrimination and that she failed to establish that the agency's legitimate, nondiscriminatory reason for her termination was a pretext for unlawful discrimination.

CONTENTIONS ON APPEAL

On appeal, complainant states that she "should have filed a religion EEO [sic]. I apologize for the age thing." She states that the SDO ordered her to work overtime on August 12, 2006, and she informed him at that time that she could not do so because she was going to church the next morning. However, she further states that she does not believe that the SDO heard her when she indicated to him that she could not work overtime. She also states that the SDO "thought he owned me to work overtime."

In response, the agency urges the Commission to affirm the agency's final decision. The agency argues that complainant is prohibited from raising a claim of discrimination based on religion for the first time on appeal. The agency also argues that complainant failed to establish a prima facie case of age discrimination and that she failed to establish pretext.

ANALYSIS AND FINDINGS

As this is an appeal from a decision issued without a hearing, pursuant to 29 C.F.R. § 1614.110(b), the agency's decision is subject to de novo review by the Commission. 29 C.F.R. § 1614.405(a).
See EEOC Management
Directive 110, Chapter 9, § VI.A. (November 9, 1999) (explaining that the de novo standard of review "requires that the Commission examine the record without regard to the factual and legal determinations of the previous decision maker," and that EEOC "review the documents, statements, and testimony of record, including any timely and relevant submissions of the parties, and . . . issue its decision based on the Commission's own assessment of the record and its interpretation of the law").

To prevail in a disparate treatment claim, complainant must satisfy the three-part evidentiary scheme fashioned by the Supreme Court in McDonnell Douglas Corp. v. Green, 411 U.S. 792 (1973). Complainant must initially establish a prima facie case by demonstrating that she was subjected to an adverse employment action under circumstances that would support an inference of discrimination. Furnco Construction Co. v. Waters, 438 U.S. 567, 576 (1978). Proof of a prima facie case will vary depending on the facts of the particular case. McDonnell Douglas, 411 U.S. at 804 n. 14.

The burden then shifts to the agency to articulate a legitimate, nondiscriminatory reason for its actions. Texas Department of Community Affairs v. Burdine, 450 U.S. 248, 253 (1981). To ultimately prevail, complainant must prove, by a preponderance of the evidence, that the agency's explanation is pretextual. Reeves v.

Sanderson Plumbing Products, Inc., 530 U.S. 133, 120 S.Ct. 2097 (2000); St. Mary's Honor Center v. Hicks, 509 U.S. 502, 519 (1993).

Assuming arguendo that complainant established a prima facie case of discrimination based on age, we find that the agency articulated legitimate, nondiscriminatory reasons for its actions. The SDO submitted an affidavit into the record stating that complainant was terminated for failure to comply with his instructions. According to the SDO, complainant failed to work overtime as directed, and she left work while on duty without permission.

Complainant now bears the burden of proving by a preponderance of the evidence that the agency's articulated reason for its action was a pretext for discrimination. Upon review, we concur with the agency's determination that complainant failed to establish pretext. Complainant stated in her own affidavit that SDO was unaware of her age, and that she did not believe age was a factor in the SDO's decision to terminate her employment. On appeal, she again indicated that her age played no role and that the SDO may not have heard her when she stated that she could not work overtime.

It is not clear whether complainant, on appeal, is attempting to raise religion as a basis of discrimination in this case or simply informing the Commission what she feels she should have alleged originally. Nevertheless, we note that complainant had ample opportunity to allege that she was discriminated against due to her religion, but she only alleged discrimination based on age during EEO counseling, in her formal complaint, and during the investigation of her complaint.

Moreover, even assuming arguendo that she had raised religion as a basis of discrimination, our decision finding no discrimination would remain the same. The record is devoid of any evidence that the agency's action was motivated by discriminatory animus of any kind. Complainant herself has stated several times that she does not believe that the SDO even heard her when she indicated that she did not want to work overtime. Thus, we find no reason to conclude that he heard her say that she wanted to go to church the next day. Accordingly, we find no persuasive evidence that would raise an inference of discrimination based on complainant's religion.1

CONCLUSION

Accordingly, based on our thorough review of the record, the Commission determines that the agency's final decision finding no discrimination was proper and is AFFIRMED.

STATEMENT OF RIGHTS - ON APPEAL RECONSIDERATION (M1208)

The Commission may, in its discretion, reconsider the decision in this case if the complainant or the agency submits a written request containing arguments or evidence which tend to establish that:

1.      The appellate decision involved a clearly erroneous interpretation of material fact or law; or

2.      The appellate decision will have a substantial impact on the policies, practices, or operations of the agency.

Requests to reconsider, with supporting statement or brief, must be filed with the Office of Federal Operations (OFO) within thirty (30) calendar days of receipt of this decision or within twenty (20) calendar days of receipt of another party's timely request for reconsideration.

See 29 C.F.R. § 1614.405; Equal Employment Opportunity Management Directive for 29 C.F.R. Part 1614 (EEO MD-110), 9-18 (November 9, 1999). All requests and arguments must be submitted to the Director, Office of Federal Operations, Equal Employment Opportunity Commission, P.O. Box 77960, Washington, DC 20013. In the absence of a legible postmark, the request to reconsider shall be deemed timely filed if it is received by mail within five days of the expiration of the applicable filing period.

See 29 C.F.R. § 1614.604. The request or opposition must also include proof of service on the other party.

Failure to file within the time period will result in dismissal of your request for reconsideration as untimely, unless extenuating circumstances prevented the timely filing of the request. Any supporting documentation must be submitted with your request for reconsideration. The Commission will consider requests for reconsideration filed after the deadline only in very limited circumstances.

See 29 C.F.R. § 1614.604(c).

COMPLAINANT'S RIGHT TO FILE A CIVIL ACTION (S0408)

You have the right to file a civil action in an appropriate United States District Court within ninety (90) calendar days from the date that you receive this decision. If you file a civil action, you must name as the defendant in the complaint the person who is the official agency head or department head, identifying that person by his or her full name and official title. Failure to do so may result in the dismissal of your case in court. "Agency" or "department" means the national organization, and not the local office, facility or department in which you work. If you file a request to reconsider and also file a civil action, filing a civil action will terminate the administrative processing of your complaint.

RIGHT TO REQUEST COUNSEL (Z1008)

If you decide to file a civil action, and if you do not have or cannot afford the services of an attorney, you may request from the Court that the Court appoint an attorney to represent you and that the Court also permit you to file the action without payment of fees, costs, or other security. See Title VII of the Civil Rights Act of 1964, as amended, 42 U.S.C. § 2000e et seq.; the Rehabilitation Act of 1973, as amended, 29 U.S.C. §§ 791, 794(c). The grant or denial of the request is within the sole discretion of the Court. Filing a request for an attorney with the Court does not extend your time in which to file a civil action. Both the request and the civil action must be filed within the time limits as stated in the paragraph above ("Right to File A Civil Action").

## A NEW DECADE

In this decade, we must recognize that change is inevitable. As President Obama communicated in his campaign, "Yes We Can". We should not be afraid to address our concerns. Ruling by fear should be obsolete. To be a sellout is the lowest form of an individual's character. Discrimination only exists when good people hurt others that are good. We must hold each other accountable from the top to the bottom. Imagine a country or world where behavior like discrimination does not play a part in our daily lives. Of course, we choose one thing over another but it should not be for morally wrong and/or illegal reasons. It is time to not just know that the laws and regulations are on the books, but also to ensure that those who have the responsibilities are certain that everyone is adhering to those established, documented guidelines mainly implemented by us the people. In this decade, if we do not effect change, when will it be done? Our children and their children deserve the right to learn how to cherish each other's diversity and live a color blind, gender blind, differently-abled blind, age blind and religious blind life, irregardless of their status. Whether you are a man, woman, gay, lesbian, homosexual, married, single parent, pregnant, educated, competent or whatever, we all deserve to have our civil rights respected.

Are civil rights on life support? The ambulance is pulling into the hospital and a gurney is waiting. The team of righteous doctors and nurses are working feverishly. The heart has been jolted with a couple of major shocks as the Doctor yells clear. And a peaceful serene silence comes over the room as civil rights opens its eyes and smiles, thank you. In this decade, we will get it right. Civil rights puts its hands together in a praying motion and says in a clear convincing voice, "Don't let this become a Planet of the Apes".

Here are website links for your convenience. You are encouraged to explore and enhance your knowledge and awareness in the areas provided.

## INFORMATION LINKS

http://www.eeoc.gov/eeoc/statistics/enforcement/harassment.cfm

http://www.eeoc.gov/eeoc/index.cfm

http://www.eeoc.gov/laws/index.cfm

http://www.eeoc.gov/eeoc/publications/index.cfm

http://www.eeoc.gov/employees/howtofile.cfm

http://www.eeoc.gov/laws/types/index.cfm

http://www.eeoc.gov/laws/types/age.cfm

http://www.eeoc.gov/employees/remedies.cfm

http://www.eeoc.gov/employers/resolving.cfm

http://www.eeoc.gov/laws/types/pregnancy.cfm

## LINKS FROM THE HUMAN RIGHTS COMMISSION

http://www.sf-hrc.org/

http://www.hum.wa.gov/

http://nyc.gov/html/cchr/

http://www.bing.com/search?q=Oklahoma+Human+Rights+Commission&FORM=QSRE3

http://en.wikipedia.org/wiki/United_Nations_Commission_on_Human_Rights

The links previously listed may be accessed as public information via the internet. I disclaim any information that you read or determine to be accurate.

Thank you for allowing me the opportunity to share and hopefully enlighten you. If this enhances your willingness to make a change in this new decade, then this was all worthwhile. It is up to you. Remember that evil and unfairness prevails when good people do nothing. Be Blessed. Following this is information on State Law from Wikipedia, the free encyclopedia.

# A BRIEF SUMMARY ABOUT STATE LAW

State law

From Wikipedia, the free encyclopedia:

In the United States, state law is the law of each separate U.S. state, as passed by the state legislature (and signed into law by the state governor) and adjudicated by state courts. It exists in parallel, and sometimes in conflict with, United States federal law. These disputes are often resolved by the federal courts.

State constitution (United States)

From Wikipedia, the free encyclopedia:

In the United States, each state has its own constitution.

Usually, they are longer than the 7,500-word federal Constitution and are more detailed regarding the day-to-day relationships between government and the people. The shortest is the Constitution of Vermont, adopted in 1793 and currently 8,295 words long. The longest is Alabama's sixth and current constitution, ratified in 1901, at 357,157 words long. Both the federal and state constitutions are organic texts: they are the fundamental blueprints for the legal and political organizations of the United States and the states, respectively.

The Tenth Amendment to the United States Constitution, part of the Bill of Rights, provides that "The powers not delegated to the United States by the Constitution, nor prohibited by it to the States, are reserved to the States respectively, or to the people."

The Guarantee Clause of Article 4 of the Constitution states that "The United States shall guarantee to every State in this Union a Republican Form of Government." These two provisions give states the wide latitude to adopt a constitution, the fundamental documents of state law.

Typically, state constitutions address a wide array of issues deemed by the states to be of sufficient importance to be included in the constitution rather than in an ordinary statute. Often modeled after the federal Constitution, they outline the structure of the state government and typically establish a bill of rights, an executive branch headed by a governor (and often one or more other officials, such as a lieutenant governor and state attorney general), a state legislature, and state courts, including a state supreme court (a few states have two high courts, one for civil cases, the other for criminal cases). Additionally, many other provisions may be included. Many state constitutions, unlike the federal constitution, also begin with an invocation of God.

Some states allow amendments to the Constitution by initiative.

Many states have had several constitutions over the course of their history.

The organized territories of the United States also have constitutions of their own, if they have an organized government through an Organic Act passed by the federal Congress. These constitutions are subject to congressional approval and oversight, which is not the case with state constitutions. If territories wish to enter the Union (that is, to attain statehood), they seek an enabling act from Congress and must draft an acceptable state constitution as a prerequisite to statehood.

State legislature (United States)

From Wikipedia, the free encyclopedia

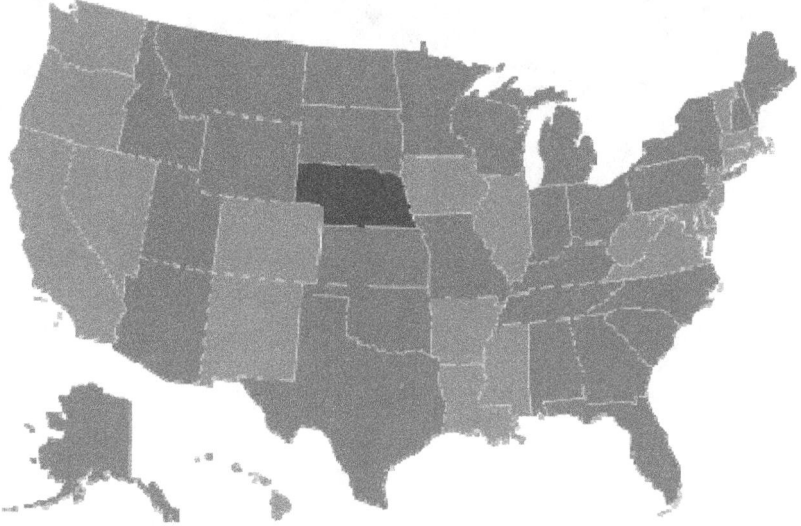

Upper chamber party control as of the 2010 general election (2011/12 session)

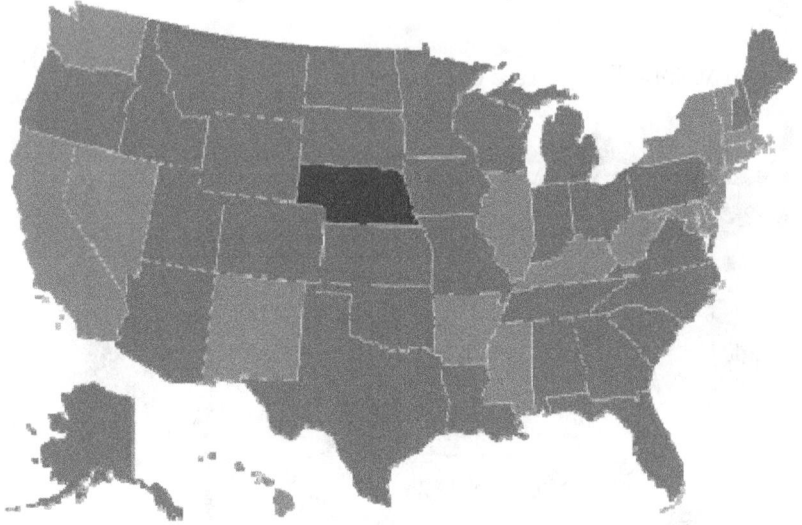

Lower chamber party control as of the 2010 general election (2011/12 session)

# POLITICS AND GOVERNMENT OF THE UNITED STATES

Federal Government

- Constitution
- Taxation

Legislature

- Congress
  - House
    - Speaker
    - Party Leaders
    - Congressional districts
  - Senate
    - President –pro tempore
    - Party leaders

Presidency

- President
- Vice-President
- Cabinet
- Federal agencies

Judiciary

- Federal courts
    - o Supreme Court
    - o Courts of Appeal
    - o District Courts

Elections

- Presidential elections
- Midterm elections
- Off-year elections

Political parties

- Democratic
- Republican
- Third parties

Federalism

- State government
    - o Governors
    - o Legislatures
    - o State courts

- Local government

In the United States of America, a state legislature is a generic term referring to the legislative body of any of the country's 50 states. The formal name varies from state to state.

In 24 states, the legislature is simply called the "Legislature," or the "State Legislature", while in 19 states, the legislature is called the "General Assembly." In Massachusetts and New Hampshire, the legislature is called the "General Court," while North Dakota and Oregon designate the legislature as the "Legislative Assembly."

# ABOUT THE AUTHOR

Sam Maze served as the Equal Employment Opportunity Affirmative Employment Program Manager (EEO/AEP) and Minority Veterans Program Coordinator at the Veterans Administration (VA) Loma Linda Healthcare System with 30 years of experience. He served as the Desert Pacific Healthcare Network 22 Lead EEO Manager for 5 VA Medical Centers that range from Las Vegas Nevada, San Diego, Greater Los Angeles, Long Beach and Loma Linda, California during his tenure with the VA. He has also served as the Chair of the Network 22 Diversity Committee; a member of the Employee Well Being/Work Satisfaction Committee; the High Performance Development Model Committee; and on the Workforce Development Council. Sam has worked for the Department of Veterans Affairs since 1987. In addition to his other duties, he was the External Civil Rights Representative for his organization as well as the Conflict Resolution Manager. He began his career in EEO while serving in the armed forces.

He started in VA as a Personnel Records Clerk GS-4 and worked through the ranks to achieve the status of Program Manager, GS-13. He is an expert EEO Counselor and has facilitated training to many EEO Counselors throughout his career. He has over 20 years of experience as an EEO Investigator. He is a Certified Mediator who was trained at the Department of Justice in Atlanta, Georgia. He provided Site Reviews for the Office of Resolution Management under the Organizational Climate Assessment Program for the Department of Veterans Affairs. He has facilitated hundreds of training sessions on the Prevention of Sexual Harassment, EEO, and Diversity in the Workplace, Mediation, Effective Communication and others. As a

Department of Veterans Affairs employee, he received EEO Manager of the Year award for the entire nation in 2002. He has received several accolades for his community involvement.

He is one of the founders of the Greater Los Angeles Chapter of Blacks in Government (BIG) and served as the president of the Inland Empire Chapter of BIG for two terms (4 yrs.) After serving two terms as the Region IX Council First Vice President of BIG, he became the regional president, which covers the geographical areas of Arizona, California, Hawaii, Guam, Nevada, the Trust Territory of the Pacific Islands and the America Samoa's. Sam is the newly elected Region IX Director of BIG and serves on the National Board of Directors who set policy and guidance to the entire BIG organization.

His main focus is helping others. Sam has completed undergraduate course studies in Business Administration and Human resources at Santa Monica City College, University of Maryland, European Division and the San Bernardino Valley College. Earlier in his life, he postponed his educational goals in order to take care of his family and is currently returning to school as a Retiree. During his 30 years of hands on experience, he achieved certification as an Investigation, Performance Based Interviewing Trainer, Customer Service Expert, Computer Operation, and is certified as a Facilitator for the Stephen Covey's "Seven Habits of Highly Effective People" course. He believes that experience and education are the keys to success.

He is currently the business owner of "Distinguished Consultant Corporation" that takes pride in serving people and organizations in the areas of mediation, training on civil rights, site program reviews, diversity awareness, management reviews, conflict management and more. *Are Civil Rights on Life Support?* is his first book project.

www.ingramcontent.com/pod-product-compliance
Lightning Source LLC
Chambersburg PA
CBHW052103270326
41931CB00012B/2872